Microservices Architecture For Beginners:

Build, Integrate, Test, Monitor Microservices Successfully

By

Joseph Joyner

Table of Contents

Introduction 5

Chapter 1. Benefits of Microservices Architecture 7

Chapter 2. How to Build, Deploy and Integrate
Microservices 11

Chapter 3. Testing and Monitoring Performance of
Microservices 16

Chapter 4. Additional Tips and Tricks 23

Conclusion 27

Thank You Page 28

Microservices Architecture For Beginners: Build, Integrate, Test, Monitor Microservices Successfully

By Joseph Joyner

First Published, 2015

Printed in the United States of America

Introduction

Microservices, or very commonly known as Mircoservices Architecture are used for describing the methods and resources that are used for architecture specification achievement. What are the steps followed or how the arrangement of all these resources is done and the design techniques that have been employed for achieving the performance goal and target cost is called as Microservices architecture. When you are looking for a right architecture to support a variety of devices and platforms, then this Microservices Architecture has been said to be just perfect.

If you are still confused about what exactly is Microservices architecture, then here is another way to understand it and that is by understanding exactly the opposite of the Microservices architecture. Monolithic architecture is the exact opposite of Microservices architecture. These are always built as autonomous units, that means just a single unit. There is a very big problem associated with these Monolithic architecture and that is any changes made to one part are all interlinked with another one. If you are making any kind of modification to some small part of the application, then you will have to make relevant changes in the other parts as well, otherwise you will end up with a lot of problems. So, this is the place where you can make use of Microservices Architecture and this is going to suit best. In Microservices architecture, small and independent modules are developed and they can be deployed or changed individually without affecting any other modules.

Chapter 1. Benefits of Microservices Architecture

In the past few years, the Microservices architecture has grown really well and there are many giant companies that are making use of it. The reason why it has grown so well is because of the small independent and easily deployable units. Have a look at a few benefits of this architecture

1.) You are going to develop, small units at a time and then deployment together, that means you will need a very less code to be written. That makes it really easy to understand this code as well. There is very less chance of errors or changes in such kind of code and if any, making changes is also easy with the microservices architecture.

2.) The process of scaling is quite simple with Microservices architecture. If you are working on Monolithic architecture, then you will have to scale all parts of the application or you will have to scale all sections. Scaling just the one that is required cannot be done, but it can be done with Microservices architecture.

3.) Anything that is really in demand today will not be used tomorrow, even if its demand is really high today. The reason is many new things come up every day and why should you still fight with the older one and some that may not suit your requirements as well. Or in case you are interested in moving to open source this is the best option you have. You will feel much more comfortable in starting something from the beginning and spending time on its development rather than checking the older one and making changes to it. Yes, this is supported by Microservices very well. As a beginner, it would be easy and interesting to start working on a Microservice from the scratch than adding or editing something already developed.

4.) You don't have to worry about deployment as well, it is pretty easy to deploy and make changes also, if in case any problem arises. You will just have to change the required part and finding that is also quite simple, which is not possible with Monolithic architecture.

5.) It is going to be pretty simple to use the best languages and tools that are going to be apt for your application. You don't have to use the same old one that you have always used. You can try different ones as well.

6.) System resilience is great in Microservices architecture compared to Monolithic architecture. When you are facing any problem in Monolithic architecture, then the complete system will not work and you will have to get a lot of things fixed. But when it comes to Microservices architecture, you are not going to face any such problem and it is very simple to get the things fixed. Only just that part is not going to work and you will not have to spend too much of time in fixing that problem.

7.) The service development team and the application assembly teams can work separately. They will not be facing any kind of problem because of this. Each development team can take care of a single microservice and then when all the microservices development is done, then you can test them and then assemble them together. This feasibility of developing both separately is something that helps in the future as well, when you are facing any kind of error.

8.) When you are developing the microservices, you are going to develop each unit separately and hence that is the one positive point. You will not face too many errors or bugs while it is running. Each microservice is tested thoroughly and then deployed and you will have to make small changes when you are deploying them together. Apart from that you will not have to do anything too much because the number of errors is going to be very less and fixing them is also not a problem at all.

Chapter 2. How to Build, Deploy and Integrate Microservices

Let us have a look at this building, deploying and integration task with the help of an example. Here you are going to see an example of an online store. Yes, when you are building an online store as a single application, then a small problem is definitely going to affect your entire store. Running a very big application in the background is definitely going to create a lot of problems for you. It is always a good idea to build your application using microservices. This will help you in understanding your application in a much better way and you will also be able to solve the problem.

Now, start building the application with microservices architecture, and you will be able to understand where could lay the problem. When you are building any microservice, then you will be able to understand yourself that it can be further split into microservices for making it look much better and also work with efficiency.

When you consider an example of an online store, that itself is a very huge application and then you should decide where it can be split. For example, you can split the shipping and handling from the rest of the online store application development. So, now split it off and then observe it very carefully. You will now be able to see that shipping is also a very big microservice and that can also be further divided into several microservices. Now, you can divide the shipping as shipping it out to the customer or to the courier services as one microservice and then tracking the shipment as another microservice. So, finally, you have orders, shipping out the order and then tracking the order, three API's to develop. If you wish, you can even further split the orders part also into many different microservices. It all depends on how well you are able to differentiate each microservice from another, so that each microservice can be built

Some people find it really different to test these small microservices, when they are used to test the end to end application. But this kind of testing is rather very simple than testing it end to end. In fact, there will be a lot of process involved in testing each microservice, but that is going to further reduce your work. Yes, when you are building a module, testing it, deploying it and integrating all the microservices as one application, you will be less like to face more problems in the future. You will have to make sure that each module is as best as possible and you will not face any kind of problems. In case, any problem arises, then it is going to be very simple to fix them as well. When you are building microservices and then integrating them together, then you should always keep doing it till all the problems stop rising.

Results of building, deploying and integrating using Microservices architecture

--- When the developer starts building, each microservice's requirement is pretty small and hence it is going to be very simple for the developer to understand it. Web container also starts working faster and hence it is going to simple and interesting for the developers also to work fast and hence the productivity is going to increase.

--- You don't have to deploy all the microservices together, you can do it individually, and hence you can make any changes to each microservice separately and as frequently as you wish to do it. You will not have to make changes to all the microservices.

Challenges that you face while building, deploying and integrating using Microservices architecture

There are a few challenges that you may face when you are developing using this approach. The first thing that is going to be really challenging for you is, you will have to decide the right place where you can use it. When you are building and deploying, you will not be able to understand the real importance of this architecture, rather the developers start feeling that it is a time consuming process and it is going to slow down deployment process.

There is another challenge that you will have to face while you are using this architecture and that is how to split the microservices. You will need a lot of experience to do this job. Splitting it too much, will generate too many microservices for the developers to develop and if you are not splitting something, then again you will have to face problems. One simple logic for splitting is to split it based on each case that the application can have.

The next challenge that you are going to face is to check the operations or the job of each microservice. When you are splitting, make sure that each microservice is doing just one job or one task. It should not be handling more than one job and if you find anything of such kind, then you can make sure that it has to be further split to make it much better and the working is also going to improve. Also, make sure that you are not splitting in such way that the task is done just partially. You will have to again work it.

There are many huge companies like Amazon, NetFix, eBay and many more giant companies that are using this Microservices architecture for their application development. So, when they are able to face all those challenges and are working really well with their applications or rather you are able to use those applications is a very simple way, then why not try it in your organizations as well.

Chapter 3. Testing and Monitoring Performance of Microservices

There are more and more companies that are concentrating on using Microservices architecture for building their projects. The reason is, it is very easy to develop simple and small microservices and the deploy them. They are, in turn, going communicate with each other with the help of API via HTTP. By using this microservices architecture, you will be able to enhance the performance and functionality for the end users. The process of testing these microservices has become a testing team as the quality and performance of the application should always be the top priority and only then you will be able to enjoy the results of using this architecture.

You will have to go with unit testing and performance testing, if you want to save a lot of time and money as well. If you are using performance testing and also load testing while building and deploying the microservices, then you can be assured of catching any kind of issue and solve it at the earliest. You don't have to worry after the application has been sent for production.

Have a look at the process of testing in microservices architecture:

Unit testing and Functional testing

At the beginning, when the developer writes some part of the code, then immediately test cases are also written for these units. So, now the test cases are run and checked to see many of these test cases are actually passing and how many of them are going to fail. Now, you will have to get the passed test cases to be checked by another test engineer, while the failed test cases has to be forwarded to the developer for making changes to the source code. Now, again all the test cases are made sure that they are working well.

When the source code for each function is written, the functional test cases are also written and testing. It is the responsibility of the test engineer to test, the test cases twice if possible to make sure that all of them are working really well. Also, make sure that the failed test cases are worked and test again till they are all working fine. Now, when unit testing and functional testing is done, it is now time for integration testing. The developer would be pretty worried about how are the microservices going to work when they are all put together.

Integration Testing

Integration testing is said to be the toughest part when it comes to microservices testing. There are many challenges that you will have to face and you should always make sure that everything is as per the requirement. You will have to decide on how to work on the bugs when something is going wrong.

Here are the challenges that you will face with testing the microservices performance

When the tests are conducted on each microservice, then you are not going to face any kind of problem. If the test case is related to the interface, it is going to be pretty easy to test it as it is not going to change more often. There will not be any kind of dependency that you will have to take care of while testing and you will be done with one by one test case with a lot of ease.

But when the process of integrating testing and performance testing is started, then the test engineer is going to face a lot of challenges. When you are releasing, you are going to add and deploy different functionalities. That may cause, some kind of complexity is testing all the microservices. Integration testing gets more and more harder when you are adding each piece of microservice. So, when one microservice is releasing an output, then the way the next microservices accept it and works on it is going to make the difference of success and failure.

Another biggest challenge relates to the microservices performance testing. You will sometimes have to test another microservice that is being handled by another team in order to make sure that your microservice is working properly.

A few things that can help you in making your testing phase much better

You will have to make use of some best practice tips that can help you in making the testing phase simple and much better than expected. You will be able to find many tips, tricks and best practices list, but here are a few that can help you as well. You will have to make sure that you are starting the performance testing phase as early as possible. This is going to help in identifying all the problems that may come up when the application goes into production. When you have identified the performance, then it would be much easier for you to resolve them at an early stage itself.

You should always keep track of the performance after the release of every build. This will help you in detecting the errors that may come up in the next build or that can also be solved with ease.

When you are going for microservices architecture, then you should first make sure that you are doing a unit test for each microservice. While going for unit testing, you should make use of only the real data that may be used by the end users. Only this kind of data will be able give you exact results and also will be able to show the exact errors as well.

Load testing is another concept that many testers miss. You should start this also in the early phase on only to those microservices where the load can be really high. You don't have to go for load testing for all the microservices that you have developed so far.

There are more and more organizations that are focusing on utilizing microservices architecture, but then the testing process has to be changed. You should never go for end to end testing and also make sure that you are taking the help of the development team for developing the test cases. When the developers are also taking part in the test case development, then you will have a lot of free time, to concentrate more on the end to end tests and that is going to be the most important part when it comes to microservices architecture.

Monitoring the performance of Microservices

One of the most important phases of the microservices architecture is Monitoring. It is very important for you to monitor the performance of your microservices. You will have to keep checking whether the microservices and also the dependencies are working as per the requirement or not. The performance of the microservices should not be hampered due to the load on them.

Many organizations are going for microservices architecture because of the feasibility to deploy and also scaling. When there are features available for making the application much interesting, you should be able to understand when that has to be done. So, when you going for monitoring the performance of all the microservices, then it is going to be pretty easy for you to take a right decision when required.

Sometimes you will have to make use of a special monitoring technique called as synthetic monitoring. This is a very useful technique and you are going to get the best out of it for sure.

Chapter 4. Additional Tips and Tricks

1.) There are many giant companies that have already implemented Microservices architecture and there are many companies which are planning to implement it. It is getting more and more popular, but if you want it to implement it, then you should first select the right project for its implementation. You will first have to start with small changes by assigning small teams to it. Making a huge or big change at once is not a good practice and most of the companies will not be able afford it as well.

2.) Try to make all the environments similar and that is going to reduce a lot of problems for you. Any changes required can be done to all and if that is fine, then everything is going to be just fine. This is not a tip for just the microservices architecture based projects, rather it can be applied to all kinds of projects.

3.) Backward compatibility has to be retained forever sometimes. You will keep adding many new microservices to the existing application. At the same time, you will keep removing the older ones as well. Sometimes, you will not be able to update those devices which are outdated and in that case backward compatibility retention is must.

4.) When you are done with the developments, testing and integrating, then you will generally forget about that project. But as a developer, who is going to work on many more such projects or even much more complex projects, you should be able to retain the project knowledge forever and especially the knowledge about the bugs that you had to fix or those bugs that were really hard to be fixed.

5.) There are many chances of failure when you are developing any kind of application with the help of any kind of architecture. When there are more failures, then you should be ready for faster recovery as well. Do not worry about the failures in microservices architecture, rather you should first concentrate more on how to recover and dividing the microservices plays an important role is making the application much stronger. Spend more time or pay a lot of attention when you are in the job of splitting the application.

6.) Your development skills or the splitting skills should never be limited to the infrastructure that is available for you.

7.) If you are the first one and only one to support the microservice architecture in your company or your team, then your attention should be more on success. You should make sure that whatever your team is working on or testing, it has to be just perfect and that is how you will be able to convince other teams as well. The number of successful microservices you will be able to show will decide your success. The numbers are going to be your best friends.

8.) It is very important to take care of the code from the first day, rather you will have to concentrate on code from first line itself. As the entire application is divided into different microservices and they are pretty small as well. So you will not have too much of the code in each microservice.

9.) Scaling is also something that you will have to take care from the day one. When you are done with testing, then you will be happy with the results that you get to see, but you should also remember that you may sometimes have to serve some millions of clients and hence it is important to be ready for such kind of scaling.

10.) Automate the entire process from day one. You can make use of DevOps for automating this complete process and it is going to increase the productivity by doing this. It is very important to monitor the results when you are going for automation process.

11.) As a developer or tester, you should always keep yourselves updated with as much information as possible able the project. You should have knowledge about development, deployment process and also about the testing phase. You should make yourself involved in all the phases of this development process.

Conclusion

So, if you are planning to develop applications using Microservices architecture, then you need to keep in mind about the three challenges that you are going to face. The first challenge that you are going to face is regarding the selection of the project that is just right for you to start the development process, the next step would be about splitting the application into microservices and this step has to be done with a lot of care and interest. When you are developing, then you are going to do this job much more. The last step would be testing and you should start this phase as early as possible to make sure that there are no too many errors or bugs coming up. Microservices architecture can be really beneficial to the companies when you are able to understand the best way to use it.

Thank You Page

I want to personally thank you for reading my book. I hope you found information in this book useful and I would be very grateful if you could leave your honest review about this book. I certainly want to thank you in advance for doing this.

If you have the time, you can check my other books too.